God's Girl

God's Girl

Rebecca Monique Rivera

MOSLEY
PUBLISHING
GROUP

San Diego, California

Editing by Karen Louise Wilkening, Expert Editing, Ink.

Interior design by Bryn Best

Interior watercolors by Lisa Kelm

Cover design by Ashley Brown

Printed in the United States of America

ISBN 1-886185-01-8

Dedication

This book is dedicated
to Rebecca's family,
especially her loving mother Mrs. Rivera;

to the caring team of the San Diego Cancer Center
in Vista, CA;

and most importantly...
to all those affected by cancer or any life-threatening illness.

Acknowledgments

Thank you, Rebecca, for being an inspiration.

This book is a tribute of love created
with help and support from
Mrs. Rivera, Rebecca's mother;
Dani Grady, Director of Development
and Institute Relations, SDCRI;
Deborah Mosley, Mosley Publishing Group;
Karen Louise, Expert Editing Ink, our editor;
Tammy Cartmel, Oncology Nurse Manager at SDCC;
Elena Garcia, *Barbara Lindstrom*, and all the staff
of the San Diego Cancer Center in Vista, CA

All proceeds from this book will be distributed among . . .

Rebecca's mother, *Becki Rivera,*
who, in addition to missing her beloved young girl,
struggles to handle a job and care for her disabled son;

the *San Diego Cancer Research Institute (SDCRI),*
a non-profit organization dedicated to finding new
and better cancer therapies and improved ways
of helping people heal through the cancer experience;

and *Hospice of the North Coast,*
Carlsbad, CA

Contents

Foreword

It is an honor for me to write this foreword for the collection of Rebecca Rivera's poems, which we've named *"God's Girl."* The title reflects how Rebecca felt about herself. She would often tell us, "I'm not worried or scared because God is taking care of me – I am God's Girl!" Even the license plate on her car read "God's Girl," and through reading her poems you will understand why.

This is an important book for several reasons. Rebecca was a sweet and wise young woman who left a legacy of encouraging messages that must be heard. Although she did write about being in love, many of her inspiring and poignant poems were written in moments of pain, fear, worry, and sorrow. Her words will touch many lives – from people coping with illness – to medical personnel and Hospice teams – to anyone who has, or had, a loved one with a serious illness. Her writings will inspire anyone who seeks to understand the meaning of their life's hardest challenges. Rebecca's words will make you think, give you solace, and strengthen your spirit.

Rebecca was a special teacher for me, and among her many gifts I am sure she made me a better doctor. I learned much from

Rebecca about life, the human spirit, and especially about courage. Rebecca taught me how to appreciate life in a special way. She made her entire medical team feel that we were making a major difference in her life and in the lives of others. She would share with me when she felt worried and scared, but emphasized that she also felt great comfort from the whole team caring for her.

From the first day I met Rebecca, I realized she was a very special human being. She was only 19 years of age when she was referred to me in February of 1997 with newly-diagnosed acute leukemia. This vibrant young lady with beautiful, penetrating brown eyes and long brown hair impressed me. Although she was somewhat shy at first, Rebecca was very sure of herself, and strong-willed. She was frightened by the medical system; she didn't want any needles, tests or treatments. After a long, gentle conversation with her, she came to understand that there were procedures we needed to do in order to make the correct diagnosis and decide on the best treatment. Rebecca had a very strong spirit and knew, without a doubt, what was right and wrong with, and for, her. Over time we gained her trust, and she put her life into our hands.

She and I got to know each other well and became very good friends. We were able to tease each other knowing we were in the same boat together, just playing different roles. I was her treating physician, with knowledge of her condition, and she was my patient, with an immense knowledge about life.

It was clear from all our conversations that Rebecca had a profound wisdom about life and the human experience. Even when she became very ill, Rebecca knew how to enjoy the simple things in life, such as sharing a smile with a loved one, holding hands with a friend or family member, and even looking into each other's eyes and seeing the connection we all share. While she was enjoying each day in this life, she was also connecting to the other side, preparing for her death. She was not afraid of dying. She taught me how to continue to live life to the fullest, not to fear pain or death, and to have complete faith in God.

Rebecca started chemotherapy for acute leukemia in February 1997 and continued until July of the same year, when she went into remission. She moved to northern California to work and continue her studies. She returned a few times for blood tests, repeat bone marrow biopsy, and to visit with us and give *us* encouragement. She would tell us how happy she was, savoring life and spending time with her family, friends and boyfriend.

On one of her visits she brought me a very special gift. She had framed a touching poem she wrote for me in the midst of her treatment. It still hangs in my office today: *"My Trusted Friend"* (March 21, 1997). This was our only indication of her love for poetry, as we had no knowledge that Rebecca wrote and kept a private collection of poems.

Unfortunately our dear Rebecca relapsed with acute leukemia in October of 1998. I referred her to another institution, where she underwent bone marrow transplantation. Despite the best medical care, she developed severe complications, including recurrent infections, graft-versus-host disease, and liver failure. Rebecca kept her spirits up for her mother, her family, and the rest of us, even though she knew, at the tender age of 21, that her days were numbered. At all times her values remained untouched, never compromised by what she endured. Rebecca died on the morning of June 14, 1999.

Rebecca's death was a great loss for all who knew her. I was devastated. I had lived with the hope she would recover and continue to enjoy life in a way that few people know. Maybe my vision was limited, only thinking about this physical life. Knowing Rebecca, she had other vistas, other places to go.

After Rebecca's death, her mother found Rebecca's collection of poems she had kept in a private folder. Some poems were saved as her favorites, but most she had written herself over the years. When I met again with Mrs. Rivera, she shared these poems with me: They were candid, heartfelt, touching. One of Rebecca's favorite poems, of unknown author, is entitled: *"For Those I Love, For Those Who Love Me."* Several copies of this poem were found among her belongings, suggesting she took comfort in its verses. Beyond Rebecca, this poem has touched many lives, as I made copies and passed it on to coworkers, physicians, cancer center staff, family and friends.

Mrs. Rivera also shared with me an audiotape that was found. This tape has Rebecca's voice praying to God, thanking him for all she had, and also asking God for guidance and help during her difficult moments. This short tape is also an inspiration and a message of faith, hope and gratitude that I have shared with my staff and some patients.

Mrs. Rivera and I talked about publishing Rebecca's special poems, as I was sure they would help and inspire many people. Time went by, and we both got busy with our lives, although we both knew this project would materialize someday.

Recently I gave a few of Rebecca's poems to the priest at my church, and he read them during mass. I was moved by the reactions around me, and was inspired to proceed with the publication of Rebecca's Book of Poems with no delay. With the help of our talented publisher Deborah Mosley, herself a cancer "thriver," the team of Mrs. Becki Rivera, Dani Grady, our editor Karen Louise, Tammy Cartmel, and several of our cancer center staff compiled this book to share with you.

These poems are not just a memorial to Rebecca. They are also an inspiration to patients and caregivers everywhere who face the constant challenge of serious illness. Now her words of hope, love, courage, compassion and understanding can reach a much wider audience, who can draw from her strength. Enjoy her writings, and know that Rebecca's spirit is still alive and vibrant, guiding us through our own journeys.

Daniel Vicario, M.D.
Clinical Oncologist
Medical Director,
San Diego Cancer Center
Vista, California
www.sdcancer.com
October 2002

God's Girl

(*Author Unknown)

God looked around his garden,
and found an empty place.
He then looked down upon this earth,
and saw your angelic face.
He put his arms around you,
and lifted you to rest.
God's garden must be beautiful,
for He always takes the best.

He knew that you were suffering,
He knew you were in pain.
He knew that you would never
get well on earth again.

He saw the road was getting rough,
and the hills were hard to climb,
so He closed your weary eyelids,
and whispered peace be thine.

It broke our hearts to lose you,
but you didn't go alone.
For a part of all of us went with you,
the day God called you home.

*Note: This is one of only three poems in this book not written by
Rebecca. They are included because they were very special
to her.

Part One

Faith, Strength, and Inspiration

I'm Thankful

I'm thankful for what I've got
Mad about this I'm not.
Even though my life took a turn
Bad memories I soon will burn.

In my mind I will not dwell
Because I know that all will be well.
So show me the things I need to do
On the road to be with You.

I Know Where I'm Headed

My heart is filled with joy
Though I'm empty inside...
I feel my heart is lifted
But I cannot touch the sky.

I know where I'm headed
Though I often get lost...
Just a price I'm paying
What a huge cost.

I try my hardest
But then I fall...
I'm doing my best
I'm giving my all.

The Love You Put In My Heart

To my Lord up above
I pray to you with all my love
I'll try and try every day
Just so I can say
Thanks Lord for the strength
You have given me this day.

I thank you for the days you've given me
Because there's nothing more anyone can give
Than another day of their life to live.

I begin to think that you're not just the Lord
But you're the father and the creator of this world
And I write this to you to say thanks again
For the love you have put in my heart
That I can give to others
So the world and its people
Are not so far apart.

I Will Succeed

I'm on my way to City of Hope
To get a transplant that I need
And through all the biopsies,
Chemo and hair loss
I know I will succeed.

God has only made me stronger
By each step he's put me through
And I've come to realize this is what
He's chosen for me to do.

I'll fight the disease not once, but twice
And show the world it can be done
That it's all in your faith
And that you can be #1.

*Note: Rebecca wrote this poem on the back of her instruction sheet
for "Dietary guidelines following high dose chemotherapy."

Angels Wait For Me

When I die
please I beg of you not to cry
because I know my time has come.

I will miss the ones I've loved
but I know that up above
where I will be
angels wait for me
greeting me with love and care
and to say they'll always be there.

The love in my heart
will never be apart
and every day will grow
for those I've loved below.

Please think of me
when I would play
with love and cheer,
and I will be here.

Don't remember me with sorrow
or I won't be here for you tomorrow.

All that I ask is
when I die
go on with your lives
and know I will be waiting for the day
when I can say
I love you
to your face again.

Be Strong

If somehow
you find out the truth...
Be strong.

If one day
your heart is broken...
Be strong.

If the guy you love
hurts you...
Be strong.

If someone
makes you unhappy...
Be strong.

If you need to cry, do it.
But if you feel you went wrong...
Then think again.

Bless My Body, Bless My Soul

I'm here in your house today
Dear Jesus, blessing the Sabbeth day.

Give me strength to come again
And not look away and turn to sin.

Bless my body, bless my soul
Give me wisdom to gain control.

I'm confused, I need to know
That special way I should go.

I need to get closer to you
Oh dear Lord Jesus, what should I do?

*Note: Rebecca wrote this poem in a Bible study class.

For Those I Love . . .
For Those Who Love Me

(*Author Unknown)

When I am gone, release me, let me go

I have so many things to see and do.

You mustn't tie yourself to me with tears,

Be happy that we had so many years.

I gave you my love. You can only guess

How much you gave me in happiness.

I thank you for the love you each have shown,

But now it's time I traveled on alone.

So grieve awhile for me, if grieve you must.

Then let your grief be comforted by trust.

It's only for awhile that we must part.

So bless the memories that lie within your heart.

I won't be far away, for life goes on.

So if you need me, call and I will come.

Though you can't see me or touch me, I'll be near.

And if you listen with your heart, you'll hear

All of my love around you soft and clear.

And then, when you must come this way alone...

I'll greet you with a smile and say

"Welcome Home."

*Note: This is one of only three poems in this book not written by Rebecca.
They are included because they were very special to her.

Take My Hand

Pain in my heart
Pain in my chest
Hard to understand
Why it will not rest.

I feel so weak
But the Lord keeps me strong
My heart wants to stop
But He carries me along.

Oh Lord give me strength to carry on
Help me through surgery and keep me strong
Guide my spirits and keep them high
Just like the angels up in the sky.

I know through you Jesus, I'll be alright
I will be brave and continue the fight
So walk with me and take my hand
Guide me through this so I'll understand.

Feet

I

start

my

earthly

days

with

both

feet

firmly

on the

ground.

Lift Up Your Worries

One day my child . . .

One day you see . . .

All things you seek . . .

Shall be blessed unto thee . . .

Have patience and faith . . .

And you'll find the path . . .

That you should take . . .

With a smile and a laugh . . .

Lift up your worries . . .

And give them to me . . .

And I shall cast them out to sea . . .

At the bottom is where they'll stay . . .

So you may find peace . . .

In each passing day . . .

Stay strong my child . . .

With your head held high . . .

For there are blessings for you . . .

Up here in the sky . . .

Follow the path . . .

That leads you to me . . .

Hear my words . . .

And they shall set you free . . .

Pick up that Book that tells you so much . . .

Feel my presence . . .

Feel my touch . . .

That is your wisdom and your strengths . . .

It will take you to heaven . . .

It's the key to these gates . . .

Life Is Like A Puzzle

Life is like a puzzle....

No matter where you go or what you do

So many pieces to solve

When you're trying your hardest

And doing the best you can

There's always someone to put you down

And say they don't give a damn.

But for me, I have not done wrong

In any possible way

So yell or scream and put me down

I don't care what you do or say.

With God on my side and the love in my heart

I know I have been good

And I've done everything in every way

Society said I should.

So you could say that I've been bad

And begin to put me away.

But in God's eyes I've been good

And He'll make it so I won't stay.

And one day you'll open your eyes to see

That this is not the girl you can lock up

And throw away the key!

When You Have Faith

I'm thankful for what God gave me
So thankful that he saved me.

He's picked me from all the rest
And decided I should be blessed.

He changed my life, turned me around
He set my feet on solid ground.

And when I feel on my own
He gives assurance I'm not alone.

I lift up my voice and praise His name
Believe in Jesus, He's not a game.

When you have faith and truly believe
There's nothing in life that you can't achieve.

When I was sick and searched for an answer
I believed in Jesus, and he cured my cancer.

*Note: Rebecca wrote this poem in early 1998 when her
leukemia went into remission.

Part Two

Family

Mom

If I could give the world to you Mom, I would.
To be able to lift those burdens away,
If only I could.

To thank you for all you have done for me.
If there was only a way
I could show you or at least make you see,
That I'm thankful
For you mom, and I'm grateful.

If I could buy a house for you to live in
I would do it in a second
And to you it would be given.

So you could have one of your own
If the world were in my hands
Not to rent, but to own.
I would give it to you
So all your dreams could come true.

When I see how hard life has been on you
All the things you have to go through
It rips my heart right out of my chest
Because for you, mother, I want the best.

But what keeps me going and helps me to see
Is that there is a better life
If only we believe.
I have faith Mom, that things will get better
If we follow Him.
We will not have to live like this forever.

On earth we are tormented by the devil's sword
But by being saved
Heaven will be our reward.
Mom, you have been a blessing in my life.
You've given me the strength
And the willpower to fight.

My Grandma and Grandpa

My grandma and grandpa
The ones I adore
My grandma and grandpa
I wish I could see more.

Even though we seem
So far apart
My grandma and grandpa
You're as close as my heart.

My Father

My father
My dad
I try my hardest
But still he gets mad.

He tells me to do this
Then to do that
He walks all over me
I feel like a mat.

*Note: Rebecca wrote "For Sabrina" at the top of this poem.

Dad

As times are getting harder
I'm becoming stronger
by just knowing ... that you're there.

As I start to think
my heart becomes so weak
but I know ... that you care.

So I keep my head held high
reaching towards the sky
because you ... believe in me.

And with knowing
it seems to keep me going
and sets ... all my worries free.

For what I've been through in the past
when I tried to keep in touch and it did not last
at you ... I could never be mad.

Because I know you're changing
and you're trying,
and just because ... I love you Dad!

I Love You So Much, Mother

I'm a happy child because of YOU!

You make me feel very loved...
You made me and gave me a life
with a happy and wonderful family.

Thanks for the love you put in my heart...
What more could any daughter ask for
than a mother like you,
so kind in the heart
and so very, very smart!

I thank you for all that you have given me...
because you didn't have to give anything.
I love you so much, Mother.

Thanks To My Stepdad

My letter of thanks goes to my stepdad Ron,
because he has been there in my life for awhile now
and he has helped me through good times
and bad times.

I'm thankful to him because
he has been a big part of my life these past years.
He has worked very hard
to try and give us kids what we need,
and for that
I am very thankful to you, Ron.

*Note: Rebecca wrote this in her English class in high school.

Like A Sister

I met someone who brightened my life.
Someone who believed in me.

She always made me laugh and smile.
And we became the best of friends.

She made me always look on the bright side.
When I had problems she took her time
and cared for me, and helped me out.

She became a major part of my life,
because I could tell her about everything.

She is someone very special to me...
She is like a *sister*.

*Note: Rebecca wrote this for Sabrina, who became her sister-in-law.
          Rebecca named Sabrina's baby, Daisy, who was born just five
          days before Rebecca died.

A Child's Angel

(*Author: Erma Bombeck)

O nce upon a time there was a child ready to be born. One day he asked God: "They tell me you are sending me to earth tomorrow, but how am I going to live there being so small and helpless?"

God replied, *"Among the many angels, I chose one for you. She will be waiting for you and will take care of you."*

"But tell me," said the child, "Here in Heaven, I don't do anything but sing and smile, that's enough for me to be happy."

"Your angel will sing for you," God replied,
"and will also smile for you every day.
And you will feel your angel's love and be very happy."

"And how am I going to be able to understand when people talk to me, if I don't know the language that men talk?"

"Your angel will tell you the most beautiful and sweet

---

words you will ever hear, and with much patience and
care, your angel will teach you how to speak."

"And what am I going to do when I want to talk to you?"

"Your angel will place your hands together and will
teach you how to pray."

"I've heard that on earth there are bad men. Who will
protect me?"

"Your angel will defend you even if it means risking
her life."

"But I will be sad because I will not see You anymore."

"Your angel will always talk to you about me and she
will teach you the way for you to come back to me,
even though I will always be next to you."

At that moment there was much peace in Heaven,
but voices from earth could already be heard,
and the child in a hurry asked softly:
"Oh God, if I am about to leave now, please tell me my
Angel's name."

And God replied, *"Your Angel's name is of no impor-tance, you will call your Angel ..... Mommy."*

*Note: This is one of only three poems in this book not written by Rebecca. They are included because they were very special to her.

Part Three

Friend

A friend is someone special.
A friend is someone who cares.

My Trusted Friend: My Doctor

A special person dear to my heart...
A special person so wise and smart...
A special person you are to me...
You are in my heart for eternity.
When I look at you, I want to cry...
If you weren't there, I could have died.

You gave me more than you'll ever know...
More than words could ever show.
Through the chemo and the injections...
Through the fears and the infections...
You have been there by my side...
Fighting this leukemia to keep me alive.

You're like an angel guiding me along...
Walking with me, keeping me strong.
I'm thankful for you and all you've done...
In my eyes you're number one.

I know you feel bad as there's more to come...
But I'm not sad, it must be done.
I follow your lead and do what you say...
You look out for me, so I'll be okay.

You are the best, this you need to know...
You have a big heart and a face that glows.
I'm often confused about what's going on...
So I ask you questions and you guide me along.

I know there's still more for me to go through...
More chemo, biopsies, and City of Hope too.
I don't understand but I won't ask why...
I'm "God's girl" so I know I can fly.

It's been a hard road that I've walked down...
But it's shown me a new life and turned me around.
It's shown how it feels to have someone there...
Someone like you who really does care.

So until this is over, until we meet again...
I'm thankful for you, my trusted friend.

*Note: Written and framed by Rebecca for Dr. Vicario 3-21-97

To Be A Friend

To be a friend is not to lie.
To be a friend, you sometimes cry.

When times you want to share,
you know your friend is there.

A friend is someone who cares for you,
when times are hard and you need them to.

When you have a friend, oh you'll know...
because true friendship will always show.

A Tear Cried For You

A tear cried for you
When I found out that day
A tear cried for you
'Cuz I had more to say
A tear cried for you
Now I know you're gone
A tear cried for you
Oh God, what went wrong?

A tear I cried
Yes, for you
A tear I cried
There's nothing more to do.

A best friend to me
I think, why you?
How could this be.
I still ask, what can I do?

I miss you, my friend.

*Note: Rebecca wrote this poem when she was 15 years old
for her best friend, Alex Lopez, who was shot and killed.*

Being My Friend

Here we go again...
I need you, my trusted friend.
Jesus came to me one cold black night
His mighty hands embraced me so tight
And with his precious mouth he said...
Everything will be okay
Go see Vicario, and you'll get through your day.

When this is all over and I've reached the end
You'll be the one I'll thank once again
It's your smile I see each morning
When I'm throwing up and sick
Your laugh I hear on the freeway
Going for treatment at Scripps.

Your strength has taught me to fight
In you, Vicario, I see a light
Shed on a life I see for no other
But the life God has for me.

So don't worry for me, my doctor
This patient will be okay
Remember, I'm God's girl...
And I will find my way.

In this little poem
I thank you once again
For being my doctor...
and being my friend.

*Note: Written by Rebecca for her doctor in 1999.

I Got A Good Deal

In my eyes,
Friend means *you*
'Cuz you've been there
Whatever I do.

You are there
Any way you can
When people talked
You didn't give a damn.

You listened to "you"
And what you believe
Doing what you could do
My pain to relieve.

You spoke from your mind
And felt with your heart
So sweet and kind
And there from the start.

No words could say
Or explain how I feel
When friendship came around...
I got a good deal.

*Note: This poem was found written on the back
of Rebecca's algebra homework.*

Birthday Card

Had no money, used up my time,
So I'm sitting here trying to bust you a rhyme.
Hope it's easy, maybe it's hard,
But I'm going to write you a "birthday card."

When you were born, you were loved all around,
Just a baby but acting like a clown.
Many days would go by, you began to grow,
Starting to mature more than you'd know.

The older you became, the wiser you got,
Starting to make decisions of what to do, and what not.
I feel you're intelligent, some may think you're not
So search down within, and realize what you've got.

Yes, life is hard, but the good times will start to roll
Then you won't always feel as if you're in a hole.

Your friendship means a lot to me,
You're cared for in my eyes
Stay sweet and special,
And our friendship will never die.

In my heart you're treasured,
In my heart you're starred
That's why you get to receive
Your own personalized BIRTHDAY CARD!

*Note: Rebecca wrote this for a friend's birthday.

Through Good Times, Through Bad Times

Through good times, through bad times
Through your feelings, through mine.
I'll be there for your feelings
Like you were there for mine.

I know you feel sad
For what you have done
But don't feel bad,
It had to be done.
No matter what anyone does
No matter what they say
My view toward you
Will always stay this way.

Don't look at what you've done
In the wrong way
Because then you'll feel badly
Each passing day.

Hold your head up high
Never put it down
And you'll see how much respect
You will get from all around.

You deserve the best
So I'll be here
To see you get the best
And never mind your fear.

I know he was sweet
I know he was kind
But it's better you're friends
So keep that in mind.

But if in a passing moment
You are feeling down
Just look for me because
I'll always be around.

Your friend always— ME

My Shining Star

My shining star is fading away.
I try to speak, but what would I say?
Through my eyes and a feeling in my heart
I sense my shining star falling apart.

I've been watching her day by day
Watching my star slip away.
Her shine becomes dimmer and dimmer.
How can she find the strength to cook dinner?

My star, my light, don't fade away.
My star, my life, you are part of my day.

I know the Lord's calling,

I see you falling,

His hold is greater then mine.

But, if I had the strength,

And wisdom and power,

I'd turn back the hands of time.

I'm here by your side,

I've been from the start.

So no need to worry

'Till death do us part.

*Note: Rebecca wrote this poem 6-30-95 for her stepdad's mother,
Ruth Alvarado, who died of cancer.

I Have A Friend

I have a friend who's there for me
I have a friend who cares for me
I have a friend I can tell anything to
I have a friend and that friend is you.

When I had problems
You where there
When I heard bad things
You made me aware.

You're a great friend
One of a kind
Friends like you
Are so hard to find.

I have a special friend
I really do
I have a friend
And that friend is YOU.

Part Four

Heartache and Love

Missing You

I sit here alone, feeling so empty and lonely...
I think of you every minute of the day...
Wondering how you are and what you're doing.

How I wish I could hold you.

I remember all we shared...
Dreaming all that could be...
And crying a tear for every minute we're apart.

Sometimes I tell myself I'm strong...
And time apart will go quickly...
Other times I cry and wonder why love must hurt this way.

Then somewhere in the loneliness...
Somewhere in the emptiness...
I find myself feeling very loved...
And I realize that it's not the loving that hurts so much...

It's the missing you.

'Cuz You Have Me

A wonderful man you have become
You've changed your ways
It had to be done
You'll show those people who always blame
And say you're still the same.

But as long as you know what you've achieved
Just walk away 'cuz you have me
Someone who knows how far you've come
You have fought the battle and you have won.
No more worries about tomorrow
No more heartache, no more sorrow.

I know there are times when everything's wrong
But those are the times you need to stay strong.
So when you're down, know I'm here
To pick you up and dry a tear.
The best of friends, yes we are
Even though I live so far.

I feel you near all the time

I guess it's 'cuz I consider you mine.

Look how close we have become

A bond so strong you could say we are one.

Always know that I am near

Never leaving, so no fear.

You're my man and I'm your girl

Together as one, conquering the world.

Love Is

Love is something two people share

Love is when they both care

Love is special, not a toy

Love is when you both share that joy

Love is when you both don't lie

Love is when no one makes you cry

Love is hard to tear apart

Love comes straight from the heart

Love is when two people try

To never let their love die.

You Say You Love Me

You say you love me, but is that so?

You said you loved me, and then let me go.

But now you're back with me to stay?

Let's see what happens day to day.

O dear Lord up above

Bless my one true love.

Open his eyes and let him see

Just how much he means to me.

What Do You Do When You Love Two?

What do you do
when you love two?
You love the one
then someone new.

You meet the second one at your house
then one day he asks you out.
You thought about it for awhile
and said yes 'cuz you loved his style.
But had you forgotten about your ex,
the one you said you loved the best?

Do you understand what's been done...
You now have two instead of one.

Love for the new guy
that no one had known
you suddenly realize
that it had grown.
You didn't know when
you didn't know why
because you still have
that other guy.

Sooooo...

What do you do when you love two?

The Promise

You made a promise you didn't keep
and the hurt inside is very deep.

I still remember the days we shared
and all the times I thought you cared.

But now I know it took too long
for me to realize we don't belong.

I remember the light in the starry skies
but the breakup was there in your eyes.

The dumb reasons you left still make me cry
but I know somehow I will get by.

I didn't know from the start
that you gambled with my heart.

I must be strong to prove it's true
that I can live my life without you.

Dummy

I'm losing you

I can tell

We started falling

Then we fell.

I love you

I really do

But *dummy...*

I'm losing you.

You Broke The Promise

You broke the promise you made
I never thought it would come to be
You turning your back and leaving me.

You said you would stay
Why did you lie?
Your broke my heart and made me cry.

I hope the girl you left me for
Gets some respect
And you don't treat her like another object.

The thing that really hurt my heart
Is you couldn't tell me
From the start.

You could have told me about her
And let me know
I would have respected you and let you go.

But no,
You had to come out with what I call a lie,
About why you were saying good-bye.

Because of Love

Problems, yes I have them...
Problems, make me grieve...
Problems, they don't seem to leave...

Problems, you're getting me down...
Problems, hear what I say...
Problems, please go away...

Problems, look around...
Problems, find someone new...
Problems, please do...

Problems, I'm praying...
Problems, I look above...
Problems, are they all because of love?

Love's Sword

My heart is crying out to you dear Lord
I feel I'm being stabbed by love's sword

My heart is being crushed in the palm of his hand
I try to make him see but he doesn't understand

The words from the winds are whispering to me
Telling me of what he's doing to me

Is this true, or is it all a lie
Why are the winds making me cry?

The feeling in my heart is telling me to keep faith
That if our love's not strong it would shatter and break.

Believe in your heart and follow the Lord.
And if your love's not smart he'll be the one stabbed
by the sword.

If all comes to an end because the winds were true
Believe in the power of the Lord to give peace to you.

I Love You

Sometimes when I'm alone and missing you
I remember the special times we shared
Sometimes the memories make me smile
Sometimes they make me cry
Sometimes they make me feel lonely
But that's not so bad...

Remembering what we've got
Makes it easier to wait for you
Because you don't seem far away.
But more than anything else
It makes me realize how much I LOVE YOU!

To Be

To be mad...

    is to be sad

To be sad...

    is to be hurt

To be hurt...

    is to cry

To cry...

    is wet, salty tears

Salty tears...

    are your fears

Your fears...

    cause you care

Your cares...

    from your heart

Your heart...

    which is now broken.

Love To Me

Love to me is simply one thing
Your love to be true
And for me to trust you.

When I pray
I ask for simple things
That only you and love can bring.

Being with you
Is like being in heaven
And no one says be home at eleven.

When you say you love me
I hope it is true
because I could never be untrue to you.

And that's what love to me
will always be.

My Love For This One Guy

My love for this one guy
Has suddenly made me cry.
People are telling me
That it was never meant to be
But can't they just wait and see?

I listened well with my heart and brain
Trying to figure out
What they're trying to explain.

What I'm going through right now
Is very hard for me.
Can't you just sit down
And listen to my side of the story?

Stop saying get a grave and dig it deep
With rhinestones from head to feet.
Printed on the stone a dove
To tell the world that I died for love.

I'm not like that
Can't you see
That's just not going to happen to me.

Give Me Wisdom

Dear My Lord Jesus
Give me wisdom to know
Should I stay with my Love
Or should I let him go?

I know we've had our problems
I know this from the past
So if I decide to take him in
Will our love still last?

I know what he's put me through
I've felt it day by day
Something deep inside is telling me
To just stay away.

But in my heart I love him
I tell myself he's mine
And when we're out together
We're like two of a kind.

So I leave it in your hands
For you to decide
Should I take my baby back
Or should I leave him behind?

What I Feel For You

Feelings so strong
They form a bond
But miles apart
Doesn't mean they're gone.

The distance is great
But the love is so near
Held deep in my heart
With nothing to fear.

It's hard to describe
The love I have inside
Freely flowing though me
Like an ongoing tide.

I miss you dearly
I miss you so much
But with your warm letters
I miss your touch.

So love me
As I love you
And together we'll make
Our dreams come true.

All In My Mind?

I don't understand you
I don't know why
I don't understand
Why you said goodbye.

But could it be
That now I know
You just wanted
To let me go?

Was it someone new
Or was it me?
Or just the way
That it must be?

I thought we'd be together
For a long time
But now I know
It was all in my mind.

You said you loved me
But how could this be
If you could turn away
And just leave me.

I shared my love
And my life with you
What more could you possibly
Want me to do?

I see how we are now
I see how it will be
So maybe it's better
That we both be free.

Love

Love is special
Love is not a toy
Love fills your heart
with so much joy.

Rebecca

Through Her Mother's Eyes

Rebecca

Through Her Mother's Eyes

By Becki Rivera, as told to the editor

My only daughter "Becca" was born the second of January, 1978 in Lodi, California. Her brother Alfredo Jr. was born 2½ years before her, Jose Fernando about 2 years after, and both her brothers adored Becca. She was a fun-loving sister, but even from a young age she "mothered" them. Throughout her life, she always showed how much she cared about those she loved, wearing her heart on her sleeve.

Becca had a romantic soul, probably inherited from me. I was only 11 years old the first time I met the boy who would years later be her father. I don't know about love at first sight, but somehow I knew Alfredo was the one for me. We started seeing each other at 13, married at 18 and began our little family right away. I call it a "little family" because we had only 3 children, while I am the youngest of 12 children and Alfredo had 7 brothers and sisters.

I was blessed with Becca...a mother's dream for a daughter. We were very close for all her 21 years on earth, and I feel her spirit with me still. Finding her personal collection of writing and poetry reminded me of each time she would show me a newly-written poem, starting when she was about 13 years old. I was very impressed with her way with words, and very proud that she shared so many of her private thoughts and feelings with me. Not all mothers and daughters have our kind of bond.

As a child, Becca was a lively, social little girl who played with dolls, loved to play dress-up, and declared "I want to be a movie star when I grow up." She was a compassionate listener, had a terrific sense of humor and she never lost it. She had a number of close girlfriends who spent a lot of time at our house and called me "Mom." Even though Becca had a very generous, giving spirit and shared me with all her friends, sometimes after they left she would look at me rather sternly and say, *"You're MY Mom!"* This 5'2" hazel-eyed Chicana never had a problem expressing herself!

I separated from the children's father when Becca was 5 years old, but she became close to her stepdad, Ron Alvarado, and appreciated him in our family. When Becca was about 15 years old and her brothers started to get interested in local gang activity, we squashed the problem with strict curfews and the attitude that "we're the family here." Becca got along well with her brothers and the three of them played together a great deal. I'll never forget the imaginative "band instruments" they were so excited to show me, made entirely of paper, right down to the pedal for the drum.

Becca was healthy and happy at home and at school, and especially with her closest friends. I remember her telling me all about the fun she had on a trip to San Felipe, Mexico, with six of her girlfriends after they graduated from high school. She was good in school, always active, outgoing and popular, but also sweet and responsible, and so I gave her a lot of trust even when she started dating.

Becca "fell in love" for 8 months when she was 13 years old, for 8 months when was 14, and for 6 years with her last boyfriend, Ruben, the love of her life. Two years older, Ruben had a good job and a good family who loved Becca. The happy young couple spent a great deal of time together and even talked about planning a wedding for the year 2000.

But there were heartaches too, and Becca wrote about them in her poems throughout her teenage years. Her poetry was always an outlet for her deepest emotions...including when she became ill.

Becca's illness was discovered in 1997 when she was a senior in high school. She had been bothered by frequent sore throats and decided to have her tonsils removed. Routine lab tests for her tonsillectomy led to the unexpected diagnosis of acute leukemia. We were all in shock and disbelief, and as a family, our lives changed forever.

Healthy all her life until now, Becca had enormous mental, emotional and physical adjustments to make about dealing with leukemia. She wanted no pity, and she kept the news from her friends as long as possible so that they would not be upset.

A great calm came over her, especially when she was referred to Dr. Dan Vicario as her clinical oncologist at the San Diego Cancer Center. He became her medical angel and a dear, supportive friend of the family. They formed a special spiritual bond, which Becca wrote about in several deeply moving poems, especially *"My Trusted Friend."* Most patients only show their illness to their doctors and medical team, but Becca shared her love, spirituality and courage over the next two years. She never asked, "why me?"

We all remained hopeful as Becca went through five treatments of chemotherapy. She never seemed to feel sorry for herself, but she was bothered when her hair came out in clumps. She said, "Losing hair is harder than dealing with leukemia," but she often dealt with it with humor. I remember her saving handfuls of her hair to stuff into her baseball cap. If some fell out of the cap, she'd just bend down, pick it up and stuff it right back in. She eventually got two wigs, and for shock value she would reach up and rip off her wig if someone stared at it in public. In a touching display of affection for Becca, one day her younger brother took a scissors and butchered off all his hair just "to be like my sister."

Our many prayers seemed to be answered when Becca went into remission in 1998. She even moved to Sacramento to stay with her father and his new family, continue her studies and work as a product sales telemarketer, and in an electric company office. She and her boyfriend were also taking a break from each other by living apart for a time.

While living at her father's home, Becca became proficient on the computer, writing and sending many letters and poems. I treasure the way my daughter expressed her love. This letter was printed with a red border and two little bears hugging, surrounded by red hearts:

Mom, How are you doing? I miss you so. Is everything going ok?

How is the family? I have been thinking about you a lot over here, wondering how you are hanging in there. I got your letters, thanks mom. I hope this one brings a smile to your face and lifts your spirits up.

Well as for me I did get the job I was telling you about, so now when I go down for my biopsy I will be insured. God has been good to us all.

I worry about you mom. It hurts me to see you in pain. I know God hears my prayers and everything will be okay. I feel it, mom.

Me and dad got baptized on 8-2-98 and it was really nice. I'm just working hard and trying to take care of me now. I'm happy mom and I'm doing fine. I still love "him" but you know how that goes.

I love you mom. I'll write you more tomorrow, promise. I'm on my way to bed. Just had to stop off and say a few words. Thanks for loving me so much...

You and me, mom, always and forever.

The humor in Rebecca's letters often made me laugh out loud:

> *Everything seems to be going fine. I've even been to the gym and by summer these extra pounds will be off. I'm down to 125 lbs now and hopefully going to get down to 110 or 115. But I want to get toned, so when I run into my ex and I'll be jogging in a G-string, he'll really be missing me! Just kidding, mom.*
>
> *But I really feel good about myself and now that I'm working out, it's even better. I told dad that since it gets so hot up here that when I get into shape, I'm going to lay out. Dad asked if I had a bathing suit and I said, "Shoot, it gets so hot here I'm going for NO tan lines." He said he would ring my neck. It was so funny!*
>
> *He tries so hard to understand me. I tell him, "Don't worry dad, I'm 20 and I know what I'm doing." He tries to tell me about the birds and the bees and I'm like, "You're a little late, dad. Mom and me had this talk years ago!"*
>
> *Dad doesn't want me to meet guys cuz he thinks the worst and says "there are too many wolves in sheep's clothing." So I tell him, "How am I supposed to find a good SHEEP unless I go out and date those WOLVES?"*

Even while she was away, Becca stayed in touch with her favorite doctor:

> *Well Mom,*
>
> *This morning 5-26-98, Dr. Vicario called me and made my day.*
>
> *I was so happy that he called. I had written him and he said thanks for the letter, and that everyone at the clinic says hi. I told him that everything was going great on my end and he said he prays for me. Also that he is thankful for me. I'm the one who is thankful. He gave me so much and a new look at life.*
>
> *It's so funny the way I feel. I miss them, mom. Not the chemo, but the people at the clinic. Doctor told me I'll only need a blood test because I feel so well. Cool... then I'll be able to sit on my butt with no pain.*

Sadly, Becca's leukemia recurred in late 1998 and she moved back to live with me in San Diego to have more chemotherapy. A bone marrow transplant she had in March of 1999 was not successful. In May she checked into Scripps Hospital in La Jolla, the same hospital where Mother Teresa had been treated. Becca's condition was deteriorating and her younger brother and I moved into her hospital room to stay by her side. I slept on the floor, giving the other bed to her brother because he had recently been struck by a truck and been left with permanent brain damage.

Becca was suffering from graft-versus-host disease, her liver was failing, and soon she could no longer eat. Her body weakened but her spirit, humor, and love stayed strong. She was the one who comforted her visitors, and even made a very stern visiting doctor laugh. Her room was always filled with family and friends, cards and gifts, religious items, and caring medical staff. Her final days were an inspiration in courage.

My daughter passed away peacefully one month later, early in the morning on June 14. We buried her on top of a hill at Oceanside Eternal Hills Memorial Park, by a statue of an angel. Words cannot express my sadness and loss, but I am comforted by Becca's poems, and by the many expressions of love from those who knew her.

My lovely daughter left a legacy of love, understanding and wisdom way beyond her years. Finding her collection of poems in several well-worn folders was a blessing, and I'm so grateful that because of Dr. Dan Vicario they are being published. I will be happy if others find inspiration in my daughter's poetic expressions of life, love and hope.

I would like to share one more precious gift from Becca. An audiotape recording was found that I didn't know she had made. She leaves us with these words from her heart, in her own soft voice:

> *I thank you Lord, for all you've done*
> *You're amazing, you've done so much*
> *Just by your loving touch.*
> *You wave your wings over me*
> *You send your angels to protect me*
> *Thank you Lord, thank you so much.*
>
> *I have a lot of burdens on my shoulders*
> *Oh Lord, I cry out to you*
> *I give you my life...*
> *I'm thankful for my wisdom, my family,*
> *For everything.*
> *My heart just loves you.*

Hello Lord, I'm here, a little teary
I've had a lot on my mind
Been thinking of a lot of things...
All you've done for me
And the life I've been blessed with...
A beautiful family...
Beautiful mom and dad, all four of them.

I ask that you guide my family and keep us strong
In your word, Lord, for that's where we belong.
Pray for my mom cause I know she misses me
I pray for my mother, I know she prays for me.
Show her the way and make her see
Oh guide her, Lord, do it for me
Take the pain from her heart
And give her peace for when we are apart.

I have so much to say
I love you, Lord
I feel your presence
I know you're here in this house
Watching over us
Giving us strength to go on
You give us peace
You give us song.

Thank you Lord, thank you so much.

Remembering Rebecca

Quotes and Photo Gallery

Remembering Rebecca

Quotes from family and friends

"Every time I saw Rebecca, she was smiling."
~Roselia Pozo (family friend)
Tijuana, Baja CA

"Becca...strong, brave...I never thought angels existed...so much pain, yet always a smile...someone to laugh with...someone to trust. When most people are faced with a problem they run, when times are bad, they hide, and when all hope seems gone, they cry. Not Rebecca...she showed me that life is a blessing and that there is no greater force than the human spirit."
~Sandra Pimentel (friend)
San Marcos, CA

"This was a special girl and I was very proud to be her uncle. She will always be loved and missed."
~Noel Lopez (uncle)
Corpus Christi, Texas

"Becca taught us that life is very precious, and to live it to the fullest no matter how tough things get."
~Diane Hernandez Silva & children (cousin)
Galt, CA

"Though no longer here, Rebecca lives within us.
~Sabrina Riora (sister-in-law)
Vista, CA

"Rebecca was the kind of person that once you met, you never forgot. Her ambition, determination and positive outlook on life's obstacles was, and still is, very inspirational to me. I am very grateful to have had a friend with such a beautiful soul."

~Veronica Medina (friend)
San Marcos, CA

"We stuck together when times were bad and when times were good, during highs and lows, with smiles and tears. Nothing's been the same since you've been gone. You may be far away but you're still close to our hearts. Words cannot describe how much you are missed."

~Nancy & J.R. Lucio (friends)
Temecula, CA

"Rebecca was such a strong, positive person. She was and still is her family's guardian angel. When she was diagnosed with cancer, she always looked on the positive side...I don't know how she did it.

I'll never forget helping to bring her newborn niece, Daisy, to Rebecca's hospital bed 5 days before she passed away. Rebecca couldn't open her eyes or speak to us, but we put Daisy in her arms and she held her. I will never forget that moment until the day I die. Daisy is beautiful and looks just like Rebecca now. Sometimes I think about how strong she was for all of us. I owe it to her to succeed in life. Strong souls like hers only come around once in a lifetime."

~Desiree Murillo (friend)
San Marcos, CA

"Rebecca Monique Rivera was my only sister. My love for her will always be. Her resting place is in my heart for eternity. I think of her every day. She may no longer walk this earth, but without a doubt she exists in memory. Her words to me were, 'Be good and strong, and always be thankful for the second chance God has given you to live'."

~Jose Fernando Rivera (Rebecca's younger brother)
Oceanside, CA

"Our beautiful granddaughter, Rebecca, was a young girl who showed her love for her family in a very unique way. We love you, Becca, and your aunts, uncles and cousins miss you always."

~Max & Connie Rivera (grandparents)
Lodi, CA & Boise, Idaho

"You're our angel, Becca. Guide us on our journeys so our families all meet again."

~David & Rachael Vanderlip & family (uncle & aunt)
Brownsville, Oregon

"I loved Rebecca like my own sisters. She always made my day. She always had a smile and loving, caring words to say. I will never forget her and the life and light that shines through her."

~Mike Sloan (friend)
Oceanside, CA

"Mija, you made our family a FAMILY."

~Amelia Ramirez & family (aunt)
Lodi, CA

"This young girl is an inspiration to me. She fought her illness like a true gladiator, and with much valor!

One day the Lord spoke to Becca and said, "I am on your side. I have chosen you, "Becca," to enter my kingdom and to give you everlasting life." Becca knew this meant she would one day have to leave her family and loved ones behind. That day came and my cousin Becca was not afraid. She embraced her illness because she knew that at the end of this long fought battle, she would triumph. She is now in a better place...Becca is now the morning sun and the evening star! Amor, eterno."

~Molly Ramirez-Jasso (cousin)
Merced, CA

"My sister, how much I love her
My sister, how much I needed her
Many times I got caught up in crime
So I had to pay a fine
And she bailed me out every time
She is definitely one of a kind
Always told me to straighten up my life
She knew I needed help
So she introduced me to my wife
My only sister, two years younger
We experienced a lot together
Rain or shine
She would smile all the time
Then one day smiles were taken away
From what the doctors had to say
Then two years later
The Lord took her away."

~*Alfredo Rivera, Jr. (Rebecca's older brother)*
Vista, CA

Quotes from the San Diego Cancer Center staff

"Rebecca was young and full of life, spirit and energy. Her smile radiated her joy of life. This smile touched other patients in the treatment area as well as the medical staff. It was an honor and a privilege for Rebecca to allow us to care for her. On the days that she felt well her delightful personality illuminated joy and laughter; on the days that she was not feeling well she showed an incredible strength and fortitude to fight her disease. After her relapse she realized that her time was short. She demonstrated great strength and courage and did not let her disease hinder living her life to the fullest. Her conversations with me demonstrated that she possessed an inner knowledge, understanding and acceptance of her time on this earth.

Although she was very young, Rebecca's soul encompassed an advanced wisdom most of us wish we could attain. As she relied on her medical team to teach her about her disease, she did not realize how much she taught us about living."

~Tammy Cartmel, RN, BSN, OCN
Oncology Nurse Manager, SDCC

"As a member of Rebecca's medical oncology team, I was initially struck by how beautiful she was. In the next instant, I realized that she was the first patient that I had ever seen who was younger than I was. Incredibly, in the midst of fighting for her life, Rebecca reached out as a friend and teacher. She taught me some of the most important ways to be a better caregiver – to keep the patient's point of view at the forefront. She was an example to all of us of how to live each moment to the fullest."

~Elena Garcia
Medical Assistant, SDCC

"This book of poetry is a beautiful reflection of a life well mastered. Young Rebecca shows us all the art of living fully in this life while reaching for the next. Her words and spirit are a treasure of wisdom and grace for everyone at any stage of life."

~Dani Grady, cancer survivor, Director of Development,
San Diego Cancer Research Institute
Board Member, National Coalition for Cancer Survivorship

"Anyone who met Rebecca could see – right away – that she was a very special person. I saw how profoundly she affected those who met her in person, and now those who read her poems. Rebecca's joyful belief in the next life challenged me to look into my own beliefs, and to be strong and sure."

~Jennifer Brown
Front Office, SDCC

"Rebecca was a sweet and wise young woman who left a legacy of encouraging messages. Her poems are an inspiration to patients and caregivers everywhere who face the constant challenge of serious illness. Rebecca's words of hope, love, courage, compassion and understanding will make you think, give you solace, and strengthen your spirit."

~Daniel Vicario, M.D.
Clinical Oncologist, Medical Director
San Diego Cancer Center, Vista, CA
www.sdcancer.com

Quote from Hospice of the North Coast

"We at the Hospice of the North Coast feel it is such a privilege to be invited into someone's world when that person is facing the last months or days of a precious life cut short by disease. It is an honor to share the intimacies involved when a patient and family are facing end-of-life challenges.

Although I didn't have the joy of knowing Rebecca while she was alive, I feel I know her well through her amazing poetry. Rebecca graciously shared her feelings and emotions through her poems, giving us insight into her life - her joys, her hopes, and sometimes her sadness - as this beautiful, vibrant young girl faced a terminal illness.

Rebecca's legacy is truly a treasure for all of us. Her poetry helps us learn that we can find beauty in a situation even when we think there could not possibly be any. We thank God for the gift of Rebecca, and thank her mother for sharing Rebecca's beautiful gift with the world."

~Mary Eacott, RN, MN, CRNH
Executive Director, Hospice of the North Coast
Carlsbad, CA

Photo Gallery

Rebecca, 5 years old

Rebecca, 2 months old, 1978

Rebecca, 2 years old, Christmas 1980

Rebecca's Senior High Prom, 1996

Rebecca and friend Luzann, 15 years old

Rebecca and friend Nancy, 17 years old

Rebecca during remission

Rebecca and the car she sold to her brother,
Alfredo, for $1.00

Rebecca's mother Becki, and brothers Alfredo and Jose Fernando

Rebecca's brother Alfredo, his wife Sabrina,
daughter Daisy and son Freddy, 2002

Rebecca in one of her wigs

Rebecca (upper left), family, and friends at the beach, 1998

Pamela, Sabrina, Sandra and Rebecca having fun

Rebecca (second from left) and her posse of girlfriends, 1997

Rebecca (far left) and friends dressed for a night on the town

Rebecca during chemotherapy

Daniel Vicario, M.D.,
Clinical Oncologist, Medical Director,
San Diego Medical Center

Rebecca at home

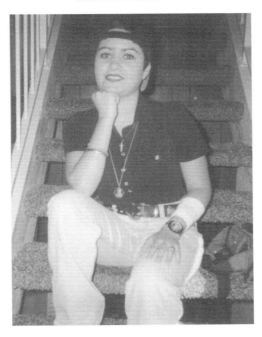

Rebecca, 20 years old, holding a friend's baby
(This is one of the last photos taken of Rebecca)

Book Order Form

(Fill out if mailing payment)

Name: _____

Address: _____

City/State/Zip: _____

Phone: (_____)_____ Fax: (_____)_____

Email: _____

GODS GIRL $13.95

Number of books x $13.95: _____

CA SALES TAX @ 7.50%: _____

$5.00 SHIPPING: _____

TOTAL: _____

PAYMENT METHOD

CHECK#: _____   (MAKE PAYABLE TO: MOSLEY PUBLISHING GROUP)

CREDIT CARD#: _____

EXPIRATION DATE: _____ VISA: _____ M/C: _____

SIGNATURE: _____

ORDER BY PHONE: **1 (866) 566-7539**   *Special price for volume purchases*

ORDER BY INTERNET: **www.mosleypublishing.com**

ORDER BY MAIL: **MOSLEY PUBLISHING GROUP**
P.O. BOX 263
WHEELING, IL 60090

PLEASE ALLOW 7 DAYS TO SHIP
INCLUDE $5.00 PER BOOK FOR SHIPPING AND HANDLING

THANK YOU FOR YOUR ORDER!